May you e?
promised
this Christmas.

*Julie Adam*

# Reclaiming
## Christmas
*Joy*

Cover concept by Meghan Crowley, Wisty Prints Art
Layout and formatting by Nelly Murariu (pixbeedesign.com)
Author photos by Kelly Burke Schackmann at Life Unfiltered Photography
Photos from Pixabay.com, Unsplash.com, and DepositPhotos.com

# Reclaiming
## Christmas *Joy*

## 25 Days of Refreshment
## with Jesus

JULIE ADEME

# Dedication

To my husband, who loves me unconditionally. You've helped me see my writing as a gift from Jesus. Thank you for encouraging me to pursue my dreams.

To my children and friends who've cheered me on every step of the way, thank you. Your words and prayers have mattered.

# Contents

# A Note from Julie

Dear Friend,

Christmas is a time for celebration. We celebrate the birth of our Savior, Jesus. We gather in our homes as we celebrate the season of giving with friends and family. We celebrate by decorating, listening to holiday songs, and gazing at the brightly illuminated holiday displays.

My Christmas also comes with a full calendar. The month fills with shopping, parties, decorating, baking—the list is endless. I desire to focus on the celebration of Jesus' birth, but each year my self-imposed plans leave me busy, overtired, and anxious. I don't want to continue repeating this cycle with no time to reflect on Jesus and no energy to love others well. Tell me I'm not alone!

Friend, there is another way. Join me December 1st as we begin our day reclaiming Jesus' promised gifts of peace and joy. Each day we will unwrap the blessings of worship and prayer by connecting with the life-giving breath of Christ. Together we will be refreshed by His love and have the capacity to share His love with others.

I know it's difficult to find time in our busy day for worship, but trust me, Jesus is faithful to help us on this journey. He will bless us as we spend time together, and along the way, our relationship with Him will flourish.

Come join me on an adventure with Jesus.

Julie

**DECEMBER**

**DECEMBER**

**DECEMBER**

**DECEMBER**

**DECEMBER**

**DECEMBER**

**DECEMBER**

**DECEMBER**

**DECEMBER**

**DECEMBER**

**DECEMBER**

**DECEMBER**

**DECEMBER**

**DECEMBER**

**DECEMBER**

**DECEMBER**

**DECEMBER**

**DECEMBER**

**DECEMBER**

**DECEMBER**

**DECEMBER**

**DECEMBER**

**DECEMBER**

**DECEMBER**

# DECEMBER

"And he will be called:
Wonderful Counselor,
Everlasting Father,
Prince of Peace."

(Isaiah 9:6)

" By quieting our spirit in God's presence, our soul opens to taste and see His goodness. "

# Taste and See

*Taste and see that the Lord is good.*
*Oh, the joys of those who take refuge in him!*
(Psalm 34:8 NLT)

Twinkling lights illuminate the sidewalk as we enjoy a brisk evening stroll. Yard decorations brightly declare the season is upon us. My chest begins pounding with excitement as my thoughts swirl of family gatherings, choosing gifts, and hope for a joy-filled time together. I sigh, a desire building in my soul for a Christmas focused more on the people I love than trying to create the perfect holiday.

We long for Christmas to overflow with special moments infused with joy and peace. But in reality, the holiday often leaves us depleted and disappointed. Our intended season of joy, gatherings, and intimate conversations is replaced with an overloaded schedule, leaving us exhausted. God's intended time for reflection on the gift of Christ is lost as our focus turns from Him to our activity-filled calendars.

The holiday season often lacks moments of quietness and peace as preparations consume our days. The world gladly draws us into decorating, shopping, and planning—all leaving us drained. God knows we are easily drawn away from spending time with Him. This is why He invites us to taste and see the goodness He alone provides. When we accept His invitation, finding refuge in Him, He refreshes our hearts and infuses us with the joy He has designed for our lives.

Slowing down and spending time with God seems impossible on a normal day, but add the holidays and . . . seriously?! We may notice our restlessness and lack of peace, but we don't connect these moods with busyness. He alone is our refuge in the worldly pace of life. His daily bread satisfies and refreshes our soul.

God sees deep into the recesses of our minds and immediately knows what we need, even before we know it for ourselves. He understands our weariness and offers help. By quieting our spirit in God's presence, our soul opens to taste and see His goodness.

Are you weary?

Share your exhaustion with God. Listen for His gentle whisper. In His presence, you will find refuge and replenishment for your soul. Today, open His Word and read more of Psalm 34. Let Him encourage and restore you with His sustaining power. By taking refuge in Him, the peace and joy He promises will fill your soul.

# Prayer

*Jesus, thank you for pursuing me each day. Help me put aside the worldly things of the season and stay focused on my connection with you. May I accept your invitation to taste all you offer and share your love with others during the Christmas season.*

" Creating space to spend time with Jesus helps you recognize His abundant blessings. "

# *Abundance*

*Now to him who is able to do far more abundantly than all that we ask or think, according to the power at work within us, to him be glory in the church and in Christ Jesus throughout all generations, forever and ever. Amen.*

(Ephesians 3:20 ESV)

Wide eyed, I am surprised by the sheer abundance of Christmas cookies filling the counter. Why did I bake so many? There are enough to share with dozens of people, more than our family could ever consume. I know I bake out of love, hence the abundance of cookies. It tickles me to watch my dad's face light up when he visits and enjoys the variety of cookie choices. He rarely receives homemade cookies, and it brings me joy as I bless him with treats to take home.

Christmas is a time when we give gifts and serve at church and in our community. As obligations take over our calendars, we can tangibly recognize all we've been doing as we seek to bless others. Yet in all the doing, we may find that our relationship with Jesus has taken a back seat. We lack recognition of His presence and forget to thank Him for the blessings He bestows. Jesus loves blessing us abundantly, and it brings Him joy to provide for us in surprising ways.

As we turn our focus to Jesus through time spent together, we allow ourselves the space to listen for His voice and be blessed by His words of encouragement. For example, when reading your Bible, has a passage stood out—enveloping you with peace when you're going through a difficult time? Or maybe a song has reminded you of Jesus' love. Or hearing a pastor's message has pierced your heart. When Jesus provides what you need in the moment, He loves seeing your face light up as you recognize His lavish love.

In this season of giving, how are you making your relationship with Jesus a priority?

Creating space to spend time with Jesus helps you recognize His abundant blessings. Set aside fifteen minutes to spend with Him. (I find first thing in the morning is best; otherwise, life gets in the way and my time with Jesus gets pushed aside.) During your time together, praise Him for the celebration of Christmas. Thank Him for His love and then give thanks for the abundance you've experienced in your life. By prioritizing your time with Him, your powers of observation increase, and you'll see His work in your life. He will grow a joyful and thankful spirit within you.

# Prayer

*Jesus, thank you for the opportunity
to celebrate your birth at Christmas.
I am thankful for your love and
mercy in my life. Help me prioritize
my time with you each day. May
I be more aware of your presence
and abundant blessings in my life.*

" When we accept Jesus'
invitation to lay down our
agenda, we receive His sweet
refreshment for our soul. "

# Agenda

*He will cover you with his feathers. He will shelter you with his wings. His faithful promises are your armor and protection.*
(Psalm 91:4)

"Come see, Gramma, come see!" My granddaughter grabs my hand urgently, desiring my full attention on her rock pile. Hopping up and down, she shows me each one, seeing beauty in the grays and browns. She is bursting at the seams with joy. The sweetness of experiencing her face light up as she shows me her creation melts my heart. Her simple words express her desire to spend time together. She wants me to put aside what I'm doing so she can show me something she finds important. Putting aside my agenda, I immerse myself in the moment, viewing life through her precious eyes.

How often do we miss Jesus' call to put aside our agendas and spend time with Him?

As we prepare for Christmas, we often become laser focused on our agenda and miss Jesus' invitation for restoration and refreshment. Our preparations disturb our normal routines as worldly disruptions pull us away from the life-giving breath of Christ. Finding a spare moment to breathe is difficult enough, let alone carving out time to spend with Jesus. Yet it's in those precious moments that Jesus draws alongside us, providing all we need to thrive each day.

Surrendering our day into Jesus' capable hands is not always easy. But when we accept Jesus' invitation to lay down our agenda, we receive His sweet refreshment for our soul. As we are refreshed, our focus is removed from our agenda and placed on the holy presence of God. By keeping our eyes fixed on Him, He equips us for loving others throughout our day.

My friend, Jesus understands your daily circumstances, your struggles, and what's on your to-do list. He knows exactly what you need today and has a personal message for you. Take a few moments to play your favorite worship song. Immerse yourself in the words—Jesus is right there with you. Allow the words to be a shelter for your longing heart. Jesus loves you! His encouragement, through the words of the song, will help you thrive through the power of the Holy Spirit.

# Prayer

*Jesus, even before I get out of bed, I want to worship you. Help me put my agenda aside and find shelter and refreshment with you. May I be fully present with those I love today. I desire to seek you when I am overwhelmed, and I want to experience the sweetness of your love as I worship and praise you.*

God nourishes our
famished spirit by releasing
His fountain of life in us.

# Fountain of Life

*You feed them from the abundance of your
house, letting them drink from your river
of delights. For you are the fountain of life,
the light by which we see.*

(Psalm 36:8–9)

Our schedules have been full with work, company, and daily life. We need a breather from the nitty gritty of the week. A trip into the city sounds like a perfect respite. As we walk in the park, a mist showers our faces, and we gaze up at the magnificent streams of water created by powerful jets shooting upwards into the crystal blue sky. The light mist refreshes our faces on this balmy day. Droplets in the air mix with rays of the sun, creating an arc of colors to behold. Drawn in, we pause, grin at one another, and relax, enjoying the majestic fountain. We needed this time to reconnect with one another.

Hydration is essential. Without water, our bodies can't survive. When we go without water, our bodies enter a state of dehydration and cry out for the water they need. We experience dizziness, and if we don't hydrate, our bodies shut down. We can also become dehydrated spiritually. When we don't stay hydrated with the life-giving source of water Christ offers, we become exhausted and irritable, and we lose focus.

Have you been feeling dehydrated?

Daily, God extends an invitation for fellowship with Him. There we experience the life-giving fountain of water only He provides. But carving out precious time to sit in God's presence is difficult at Christmastime. He knows we believe everything is a priority as we prepare to celebrate. Yet growing our relationship with our heavenly Father requires time together.

Find a place to sit with God today. Inhale deeply, hold, now exhale. Allow your body to relax. Share what's on your mind. A journal is helpful for recording any impressions you receive from God. As you share, God helps you change your perspective on your worries and priorities. He alone rehydrates you through the power of the Holy Spirit.

God delights in His time with us. He nourishes our famished spirit by releasing His fountain of life in us. True lasting joy comes as we get to know Him better. As He rehydrates our souls, we shine for Him with a smile, a word of encouragement, or a helping hand in His name. As God's children, we've been given the power of the Holy Spirit to be a light to those we love. All we need to do is be present at His table to receive His gift.

# *Prayer*

*Jesus, help me prioritize my time as Christmas nears so I can sit at your table in fellowship with you. Thank you for your promised abundance and for the nourishment you provide. Fill me with your power so I may share your love and be your light to those I encounter today.*

**"** By spending time in God Word, along with prayer, we experience the lasting joy and contentment found only in Him. **"**

# Milk and Cookies

*Like newborn babies, you must crave pure spiritual milk so that you will grow into a full experience of salvation. Cry out for this nourishment, now that you have had a taste of the Lord's kindness.*

(1 Peter 2:2–3)

Ingredients are strewn across the counter as little hands help measure and mix, leaving behind a layer of stickiness. Anticipating the sweet tastes to follow, we prepare the pans for the oven. Jiggling with excitement as the sweet aroma permeates the air, we long to taste the creations we've labored over. Finally, we grab a couple of warm cookies and a glass of cold milk. As we savor our cookies, I take in the scene around the table, grateful for the memories we're creating together.

We've all experienced longing. We long for better days, peace, health, fulfillment, or deeper relationships. But have you ever longed for something more after reading a passage of Scripture? You sense God is reaching down, touching your soul, but you don't know how to process your emotions.

I'm familiar with this same longing. After reading a passage of Scripture and knowing God's trying to get my attention, I have been unsure what I should do. Usually, my mind begins swirling with the pressures of my upcoming day, and I choose avoidance over reflection. I end up walking away, but then I'm left with a realization I've missed something God wanted to share.

God's desire is to develop an engaging relationship with us that includes honest conversations about Him and our lives. No burden or confusion is unimportant. Often, reading our Bibles is the first step in developing this relationship. But if we don't engage in the conversation, we are left longing for something to fill the deep recesses of our souls—a place only God can enter.

Prayer, along with reading Scripture, satisfies the longing in our souls more deeply than doing either alone can. As we do both together, our relationship with God deepens. He quiets our souls while opening our minds so we hear Him more clearly, thus forming a deeper personal connection to our heavenly Father.

As you approach God in prayer, ask Him what He is sharing with you through His Word. Voice any confusion you're feeling. Pray for His help as you process your emotions. He will open your mind so you hear His gentle whispers of encouragement and love. By spending time in His Word, along with prayer, we experience the lasting joy and contentment found only in Him.

# Prayer

*Lord, I desire to develop a deeper relationship with you, but I don't know how. Help me talk with you as if I were talking with a friend. I want to know you better and be in your presence. Teach me to quiet the noises in my mind so I hear your gentle whispers.*

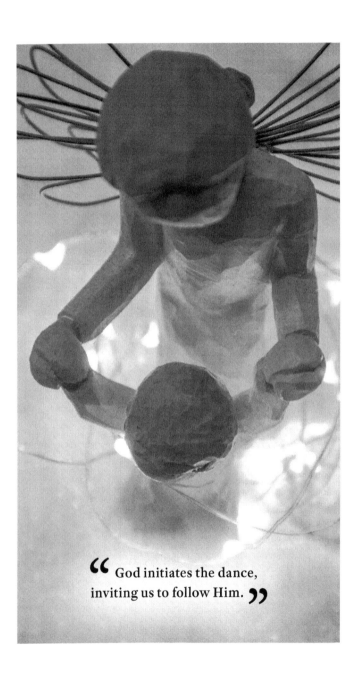

" God initiates the dance,
inviting us to follow Him. "

# God Leads and Restores

> *The Lord is my shepherd; I shall not want.*
> *He makes me lie down in green pastures.*
> *He leads me beside still waters. He restores my*
> *soul. He leads me in paths of righteousness*
> *for his name's sake.*
>
> (Psalm 23:1–3 ESV)

Laughing as we dance, I step on my husband's toes. His eyes sparkle with amusement. I have forgotten, yet again, to allow my husband the pleasure of leading. He patiently redirects me, safely avoiding a near collision. He gently reminds me: when dancing, it is his pleasure to lead. I need reminders when we dance. When I forget that his job is leading, it's hilarious. I can't always be in control. Releasing myself into the care of another, even when it is my trustworthy husband, is difficult.

What area of your life do you struggle to allow God to lead?

When God leads us into a place of peaceful stillness, we often resist. We prefer motion, having evidence of our accomplishment, especially when preparing for Christmas.

And yet when we allow ourselves to enter the peaceful stillness of His presence, we give Him the pleasure of restoring peace in our souls. Releasing ourselves into His care is not easy, but this is the place where He leads us so we may catch our breath, slow the dance of life, and receive the peace He offers.

God, as our Good Shepherd, desires to lead the way in our daily lives. He initiates the dance, inviting us to follow Him. As we follow, our lives become richer. He knows we have commitments, but He also knows how much better each day is when we allow Him the pleasure of leading the way.

Take time this morning and be still. Experience the richness He provides. Surrender your day to His loving hands. Ask Him what you should set aside today so you'll be available to love and be loved. His hand is reaching out for yours today, asking for this dance.

This season allow God to lead the way. You may need to let go of some "things" you think are necessary. But, when you come and sit beside those still waters, accepting His precious gift of time together, you will overflow with joy and have more love to give this Christmas.

# *Prayer*

*Jesus, thank you for your gentle leading, for being my Good Shepherd. Lord, help me surrender my day into your capable hands. As you guide my steps, I pray I joyfully follow your lead and experience the peaceful stillness you offer and be restored.*

**"** A Sabbath rest allows our souls to be replenished by the life-sustaining water of Jesus. **"**

# Sabbath

*As the rain and the snow come down from heaven, and do not return to it without watering the earth and making it bud and flourish, so that it yields seed for the sower and bread for the eater, so is my word that goes out from my mouth: It will not return to me empty, but will accomplish what I desire and achieve the purpose for which I sent it.*

(Isaiah 55:10–11 NIV)

Blustery winds swirl the gently falling flakes as if God were shaking the world. With the backdrop of the yard light, I have the sensation of looking out from within a snow globe. Watching the snowfall while snuggled up all cozy and warm, we enjoy the rest the storm brings. Eventually, our family will shovel the driveway, but for now, we hang out under blankets, reconnecting and enjoying a weather-forced Sabbath.

During winter, not much grows in the Midwest. The grass goes dormant, trees lose their leaves, and flowers no longer bloom. The ground takes a forced sabbatical. The soil, resting from the seasonal growth, rejuvenates below the layer of frost. In the spring, warming weather melts the snow and the seasonal rains begin. The soil brings forth a myriad of colors as the ground reawakens.

Just as the ground needs time to rest in winter before reawakening to yield its beauty and fruit, we also need rest for the replenishment of our tired and weary souls. A Sabbath rest allows our souls to be replenished by the life-sustaining water of Jesus. He provides the strength necessary for the week ahead.

Will you create space in your life for a Sabbath rest?

Your Sabbath needn't be on a Sunday, but it is important you set aside a day from "work" for rest, play, and worship of Jesus. You can do this as a family. Start your day with prayer, reconnecting with Jesus. Praise Him for who He is and give thanks for His gift of salvation. Ask Him if something is keeping you from growing in your faith. Then open your Bible and pray Psalm 63:1–8 back to God.

After you've spent time in prayer, what activity will you do today? Play in the snow, watch a movie, play a game, or bake cookies together. Put your work down and go delight in the gift of life!

# Prayer

*Jesus, thank you for creating a Sabbath. I am grateful for the time to rest and worship you today. You are the provider of life-sustaining water that helps me flourish and live life to the fullest. You alone satisfy my thirsty soul. May I worship you and praise your name this Christmas.*

Jesus' love, extended to us, illuminates our hearts and minds.

# Illuminate

*You are the light of the world—like a city
on a hilltop that cannot be hidden. No
one lights a lamp and then puts it under a
basket. Instead, a lamp is placed on a stand,
where it gives light to everyone in the house.*

(Matthew 5:14–15)

Large, wet, fluffy flakes gently fall from the sky, clinging to the trees and bushes. There's a calm in the air as a bright winter wonderland is created, flake by flake, accumulating on every surface the eye can see. Snow-covered lights glow from the bushes, the snow adding depth to their illumination, increasing their intensity and making them shine brighter than before.

Jesus is God's gift of light for our weary world. His light is an expression of God's intense love for us, so we no longer need to walk in darkness. Jesus calls each of us by name so we can experience the light He alone offers. The more we come to know Jesus, the more His light shines with intensity in our lives.

Time spent with Jesus helps us experience His love. He helps us refocus and gain a fresh perspective on what really matters. His love, extended to us, illuminates our hearts and minds, and we become less "season" focused and more people focused.

Who in your life could use the light of Jesus' love?

Opportunities surround us to share the light of Jesus with others we know and love. There are people in our neighborhoods, workplaces, and even families who don't know about the light Jesus offers. They may have never recognized the goodness of the Lord in a tangible way. Jesus invites us to participate in illuminating the darkness in the lives of others.

Let the lights of Christmas be your reminder to ask God who needs a touch of His love. As your act of worship, be aware of your surroundings. Keep your eyes open for someone who needs the light of God's love. Smile at the grocery store worker. Share a kind word with a neighbor. Write a note of encouragement to a friend. Your act of love will shine God's light into the life of someone who may be lonely this season. You can help them experience the joy of life with Jesus through your words.

# Prayer

*Lord, thank you for your
Son and His promised light.
Help me become aware
of someone in my life who
needs to experience your love.
As my act of worship, use me
to shine your light into their
lives and point them to you.*

" Jesus' deep well of love never runs dry. "

# Reservoir

*Jesus answered, "Everyone who drinks this water will be thirsty again, but whoever drinks the water I give them will never thirst. Indeed, the water I give them will become in them a spring of water welling up to eternal life."*

(John 4:13–14 NIV)

Finding comfort holding my first cup of the morning, my hands warm as I savor the aroma. My mind begins waking up. As part of my self-care routine, I normally make a second cup of coffee and grab my Bible and journal to spend time with the Lord. Our automatic coffee machine grinds the coffee beans and, on occasion, displays the message "Fill Water Tank". This message makes me cringe because routinely there are more messages regarding the care of the machine. More often than not, "Fill Beans" or "Empty Grounds" follows—not the way I like starting my morning. I simply want to get my day moving.

How is your level of care for yourself? Are you running dry, in need of your tank to be refilled by the living water of Jesus?

When Jesus seeks out a Samaritan woman by the well, He asks her for a drink. During their interaction, He reveals He is the only source of living water, and whoever comes to Him never thirsts. He tenderly shares how she will continue thirsting and be unsatisfied with life if she follows her current lifestyle. He meets her in the midst of her pain, sharing His deep well of love never runs dry. The same is true for us. As we accept Jesus as our Savior, we, too, can draw upon His well repeatedly. He fills our reservoir with His life and strength through the power of the Holy Spirit.

With Christmas approaching and many of us running on empty, what would your day be like if you turned to Jesus each time you felt tired? Lifting each of those moments in prayer, I imagine He beams with joy as He hears from you throughout the day. Answering your prayers, He will fill you with His strength and living water to sustain you each time you ask. As you receive His gift, you will bubble over with His love, enabling you to share this love with those you encounter today.

# Prayer

*Lord, this is the day you have made. May I rejoice and be glad. Thank you for calling me your child. I am grateful your words declare your unfailing love. I put my trust in you. Today, show me the way I should go, for I entrust my life into your hands. Thank you for your gift of living water. I need a fresh infusion today. Help me follow you closely and proclaim your love to the people in my life.*

"God knows we need rest and spiritual refueling."

# Rest

*Jesus said, "Let's go off by ourselves to a quiet place and rest awhile." He said this because there were so many people coming and going that Jesus and his apostles didn't even have time to eat.*

(Mark 6:31)

Caught up in my shopping, I squeeze in another errand on my way home. In my rush at the checkout, my indifference for the cashier is apparent. As she pastes on a smile, God nudges me to see the woman before me. Though she's smiling, her eyes give her away. She's weary. Taking a deep breath, I say hello and let her know I see her weariness. Grateful she's been noticed, she admits her exhaustion. I respond with a prayer for God's provision of rest, and I wish her a blessed day.

As we rush about preparing for Christmas, we often become tired. Wrapped up in our lists, we're too busy to pause and observe what's happening around us. We skip lunch, stay up late, and lose patience, and it causes us stress and crankiness.

How did we end up stressed during this season of gatherings and celebrations?

We lack the rest our minds and bodies need. Jesus prioritized time alone with His heavenly Father and was refreshed. I know you're wondering, *When am I going to find time alone?* Trust me, you will be blessed by taking time for a break. Today, shake up your routine. Take a ten-minute power nap in the middle of the day. (If you can't nap, unplug for from technology and find a space alone.)

Grab a blanket, curl up on the couch, and silence your phone. Simply be in God's presence. Close your eyes and slow your breathing. Ask Him for a fresh perspective this Christmas. Let Him remind you of His love for you and allow Him to calm your spirit.

This simple practice alters our focus and priorities. God desires us to be purposeful in our preparations rather than move at a frantic pace. He calls us to share His love in our homes and with others we encounter during our day. By resting and refueling, we can truly "see" those we encounter. God blesses those few minutes spent together by sustaining us and bringing us joy. He knows we need rest and spiritual refueling, especially during this hectic season. He sees our need for the replenishment He alone provides. Accept His offer for rest in His peaceful presence.

# Prayer

*Jesus, thank you for your example
to rest. I'm not good at resting and
caring for myself. Help me understand
the value of self-care. As I rest, I pray
you refuel my body and nourish my
soul. May I experience renewal as
you envelop me with your love.*

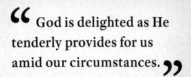 God is delighted as He tenderly provides for us amid our circumstances.

# Foggy Thinking

**11**

*Give your burdens to the Lord, and he will take care of you. He will not permit the godly to slip and fall.*

(Psalm 55:22)

Driving to church, the morning glow illuminates the sky, obscuring my view. Warm air and snowy ground have together created an eerie glow as fog rises around me. Reducing my speed I inhale to slow my racing heart, "Lord, clear the path before me so I can safely see." Pulling over in a parking lot, I wait for the fog to lift. Suddenly, a full spectrum of reds and oranges lights the sky, and the warm glow of God's love envelopes me. Grateful, I say a prayer of thanks for the safety God provided.

Fog makes it difficult to see, creating a barrier to moving forward. Burdens also create barriers in our thoughts and decision-making. Illness, family unrest, loss, and even Christmas can be burdens we are bearing alone. When we bear our burdens alone, we live in a mental fog, exhausted, and we can't detect the presence of Jesus.

What burdens are you bearing this Christmas?

When I bear my burdens alone, I lose sight of God and of how much He loves me. I can't make Him out clearly, I forget to pray, and I don't recognize His provisions or presence. This is not how I want to live, nor is it God's desire for my life.

We were never meant to bear our burdens alone. God understands the weight we are shouldering and eagerly waits for us to share them in prayer. As we release them into His care, our eyes are opened so that we recognize His loving provisions.

One of the greatest joys of following Christ is knowing He waits with open arms for us to share the burdens weighing us down. I can only imagine His pleasure when we share our struggles with Him. God is delighted as He tenderly provides for us amid our circumstances.

Personalize today's prayer from Ephesians and pray the words back to Jesus. Be an observer, searching for His provision and presence throughout your day. He tailor-makes reminders of His presence just for you.

# Prayer

*I pray that from his glorious, unlimited resources, he will empower you with inner strength through his Spirit. Then Christ will make his home in your hearts as you trust in him. Your roots will grow down into God's love and keep you strong. And may you have the power to understand, as all God's people should, how wide, how long, how high, and how deep his love is. May you experience the love of Christ, though it is too great to understand fully. Then you will be made complete with all the fullness of life and power that comes from God.*

(Ephesians 3:16–19)

**"** Praising God through song changes our perspective. **"**

# Perspective

**12**

*Praise him with a blast of the ram's horn;*
*praise him with the lyre and harp!*
*Praise him with the tambourine and dancing;*
*praise him with strings and flutes!*
*Praise him with a clash of cymbals;*
*praise him with loud clanging cymbals.*

(Psalm 150:3–5)

I need a walk after spending the week with missionaries who serve a community devastated by the AIDS crisis. I am struggling to understand the depth of their joy as they praise and worship God through song each morning. Walking along their prayer path, I enter a wide-open field full of wildflowers. I feel at peace here and stop to play worship music on my phone. Letting the words soothe my soul, I begin swaying to the music. I reach my arms upwards, singing along and praising the Lord my God. Tears begin rolling down my cheeks as the lyrics help me hear expressions of love from the God who created me. I've never experienced His presence and love in such an emotional and deeply personal way. Praising God for

His unconditional love and patience with me, I begin to understand the joy the missionaries find as they tirelessly serve each day.

Might you need a fresh perspective of Jesus and Christmas today?

There have been seasons in my life when I've focused solely on one practice of spending time with Jesus. For example, I've mainly read my Bible without realizing there are other ways to experience the character and love of our Savior. I'm not advocating ditching your Bible, but I am wondering if you desire to gain a broader perspective of Jesus and experience the tenderness of His love.

Sometimes we should shake up our routines and try something new. Instead of sitting down with your Bible this morning, listen to worship music. Don't get immersed in the beat, but truly listen to the words in the songs. The message of God's faithfulness and love are woven throughout old hymns and in our contemporary Christian music.

Music is powerful, creating waves of emotion in us. Sometimes we experience either a foot-stomping joy, a sense of reverence, or a river of tears, depending on the song. Praising God through song changes our perspective. Our singing and praising become deeply personal, holy moments between our Savior and us. As we sing, giving our whole being to Him, our perspective changes, our heart rate slows, and our eyes open to His tender love. In that moment, peace can be claimed—a peace that only comes through Jesus.

# Prayer

*Jesus, open my eyes. Show me new ways to draw closer to you. As I praise you through music, clear my mind to hear the words of the songs. May my act of worship bring you joy. As I sing the words of praise, create in me a desire for a deeper relationship with you.*

**❝** A humble spirit helps us become more aware of God's presence in our lives. **❞**

# Posture

*Come near to God and he will come near to you.*
*Humble yourselves before the Lord, and he*
*will lift you up.*

(James 4:8, 10 NIV)

As I glance out my dad's kitchen window in the Northern Wisconsin woods, I notice an animal in the distance. Tail feathers spread wide, he struts about, turning so the females can glimpse the majestic arc of his tail. The male turkey uses this posture to show his size and prowess. He makes his presence known, hoping to attract their desire. This is the way he grows his harem and lineage. Puffing himself up is instinctual—by drawing attention with the size of his tail, he raises himself above his rivals. Posturing is part of creation's mating season.

When I was younger, it was important I create the perfect Christmas. I had an image of what Christmas should look like and falsely believed an unforgettable experience equaled success. In my pride, I focused on my accomplishments, and I fell short of my expectations. I, too, was posturing, puffing myself up and creating an appearance that didn't match reality.

Posture matters. Approaching God with humility requires recognizing our imperfections and need for guidance. As we do, the line of communication is opened, and it becomes easier to pray on a daily basis. A humble spirit helps us become more aware of His presence in our lives and creates in us an increasing desire to be near Him.

How do you approach God each day?

Daily prayer needn't be complicated. It's about having a heart-to-heart with the God who deeply loves us and desires to spend time together. Pray in the shower or on a walk, or humbly get down on your knees and share what's keeping you awake at night. Create a rhythm of prayer that fits into your lifestyle. I pray in the mornings when I am more focused and less distracted—sometimes on my knees, other times with my palm up and open. As you incorporate a daily practice of prayer in your life, you will experience an increasing desire to spend more time throughout your day talking with God.

God wants to walk through your life with you and not be on the sidelines. As you talk with Him, He provides refreshment, replenishing you so you can approach your day with a posture of joy. His love flows through your prayers, opening you up to hear the Holy Spirit as you share the love of Christ with those you encounter.

# Prayer

*Lord Jesus, help me approach you*
*in humility. Increase in me a desire*
*to talk with you and invite you*
*into my daily life. Help me find*
*creative ways for prayer and make*
*it a priority each day. Thank you*
*for being my Shepherd and guide.*

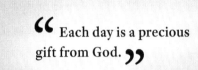

" Each day is a precious
gift from God. "

# Play

*Give thanks to the Lord, for he is good!*
*His faithful love endures forever.*
*This is the day the Lord has made.*
*We will rejoice and be glad in it.*

(Psalm 118:1, 24)

Pristine white snow blankets the ground, beckoning us outdoors. Gathering our sleds, my family gears up for an afternoon adventure. Deep powdery snow, cool crisp air, and a large hill bring out our competitive juices. Flying down the steep hill, snow pelting our faces, we race against each other. Tears streaming down our faces from the cold, we crash as we each try to win the race. Age doesn't matter as we roll off our sleds, ready for the next race.

Play is a gift from God. He created our world for delight, and in His Word He encourages us to enjoy and play. He smiles as He watches us put aside responsibilities to engage in an activity that brings us joy. Joy and laughter are two emotions that bring peace and an emotional release, together reminding us of the precious gift of life.

When was the last time you played?

Each day is a precious gift from God. Though we have necessary work that we must accomplish during the week, God has designed a Sabbath day for rest. A day for us to worship and celebrate who He is and His presence in our life. This also provides us the opportunity for recharging mentally and physically. Let's celebrate His gifts by having some good old-fashioned fun. He delights in our play. I can think of no better way to worship and celebrate than playing together as a family.

Sledding has always been a part of our Christmas celebration. Time together—laughing, joking, and flying down the hill—creates holy moments, deepening the bonds of our family. Through play, we form lasting memories. I imagine God's face glowing with joy as we celebrate life.

Today, I pray you'll schedule something fun into your day. Put on your outdoor clothes and take a walk in the park or in your local forest preserve. Plan an indoor adventure or treasure hunt. Whatever brings you joy, be intentional about building it into your day.

# Prayer

*Jesus, I am grateful you created the practice of having a Sabbath. I am excited to spend time worshipping you through play. You are a good God who has the best intentions for my life. Help me let go of my schedule, and teach me how best to create space for relaxation and play in your presence.*

" To receive Jesus' promised peace and sense His presence, we must draw near to Him. "

# Senses

*The Lord is near. Do not be anxious about anything, but in every situation, by prayer and petition, with thanksgiving, present your requests to God. And the peace of God, which transcends all understanding, will guard your hearts and your minds in Christ Jesus.*

(Philippians 4:5–7 NIV)

Stirring in my sleep, I open one eye to see the clock. It's early. My body is restless, and I worry I'll wake my husband. I rise to sit in the quiet of the morning and spend time in prayer. I grab my Bible and open the curtains. There's an orange glow across the horizon. Hearing the hoot of an owl, I ease open the door. Carefully stepping onto the snowy deck, I make out an owl perched on the neighbor's roof. As it swoops down, homing in on breakfast, I'm amazed as it senses its prey with so little light.

During the stress of Christmas, it can be difficult to sense the nearness of Jesus in our lives. Our preparations push away thoughts of Jesus as we power through the day. We can go days without a single thought of Jesus as our focus fixes on our holiday preparations. Suddenly we find we're stressed and anxious, without the joyful spirit we were hoping for.

When was the last time you thought about Jesus?

To receive Jesus' promised peace and sense His presence, we must draw near to Him. We can't keep Him at a distance. By creating space in our morning for prayer and thanksgiving, our awareness of His presence is clearer throughout the day.

I find four steps help me create space in my soul as I seek Jesus. As you practice them, I pray you experience Jesus with a fresh sense of awe and wonder.

☩ Inhale, exhale. One more time: inhale...exhale.

☩ Close your eyes and open your hands, palms up.

☩ Pray: Here I am, Lord. I wish to know you better. May your love help me be more aware of you today.

☩ Then sit quietly for a minute and experience the silence, listening for His quiet voice.

This quiet act of surrender changes our focus from our holiday preparations and fixes it on Jesus. As we pray, we move from a casual relationship to a personal relationship with the God who loves us. This is where Jesus meets with us and we become more at ease with prayer.

# Prayer

*Jesus, may I come to you with a
surrendered heart, eyes wide open,
up close and personal. My desire is
to focus on you and not on all my
preparations. May you guide my day,
and as I follow you, I pray you'll fill
me with your love and peace so I can
share your love with those around me.*

" Scripture is filled with tools to help us flourish and live a joy-filled life as His child. "

# Tools

*The Lord is my rock, my fortress, and
my savior; my God is my rock, in whom
I find protection. He is my shield, the
power that saves me, and my place of safety.
Your word is a lamp to guide my feet and a
light for my path.*

(Psalms 18:2; 119:105)

Midwest winters bring occasional days of brutally cold temperatures. The cold air settles in your lungs and your breath comes out in a fog. The cold seeps into your bones as your fingers stiffen. If you must venture out, you take warm boots, a fully charged cell phone and leave an emergency kit with a blanket, hat, and gloves in the car. All are life-saving tools necessary for warmth if you become stranded.

What's in your emergency tool kit? Maybe you have a jack, cell phone charger, tissues, and tire pressure gauge. You're prepared with tools that help you if you become stranded and need to wait for assistance. There's reassurance in knowing you're ready in case of an emergency.

Christmas is a time when we prepare our hearts to celebrate the birth of Jesus. Dusting off our Bibles, we seek wisdom and peace from its words. Scripture is filled with tools to help us flourish and live a joy-filled life as His child. It shows us how to love Him and provides encouragement when we're stressed. We learn about His gift of forgiveness and about worship and praise.

What tools do you have in your toolbox that help you flourish in life?

One tool we all use is a calendar. It is essential for keeping our days ordered, but it doesn't help us flourish spiritually. God's Word helps us live flourishing lives as His children. His Word provides examples of how to pray, worship, love others, and develop a personal relationship with Him. He wants us to share every area of our lives with Him, from the mundane to the difficult. As we spend time with Him, growing our relationship, He helps us find joy in our daily circumstances.

God's Word is the perfect gift for unwrapping during Christmas. Inside you will find tools to help you live a flourishing life in the hands of the God who loves you. Today, turn to Him in worship and praise, thanking Him for His promise of living life in His loving hands. Read Ephesians 6:13-18 for the tools God promises you as His child.

# Prayer

*Jesus, thank you for the wisdom
and promises I find in your words.
Help me create space in my day
to spend time with you. I want to
know you better and desire a life
that flourishes with you as my God.*

> Jesus changes your priorities, infusing you with the light of the Holy Spirit.

# Vessel of Light

*We now have this light shining in our hearts, but we ourselves are like fragile clay jars containing this great treasure. This makes it clear that our great power is from God, not from ourselves.*

(2 Corinthians 4:7)

When our children were young, I'd volunteer in their classrooms and help with art projects. At Christmas, their favorite craft was creating candleholders from baby food jars. The children patiently glued colored tissue paper around the jars, covering the entire surface. Proud of their artwork, they were eager to get home and put a candle inside so they could see their creation aglow. Once home, we'd place a votive inside, go into a dark room, and light the candle. As the flame took hold, we'd all gasp with awe as a spectrum of color reflected on the walls. One little light in the darkness changed the room.

What changes would you like to see happen as you prepare for Christmas? Instead of focusing on our list, wouldn't it be wonderful if we were shining the light of Jesus' love?

There is freedom and joy in knowing Jesus didn't create us to complete tasks. He created us for relationships. It isn't important if our house is clean or if everything is perfectly decorated for Christmas. He cares about you and all the messiness that comes with your life. He desires intentional time together, not being part of your to-do list.

Change is hard! Life pulls us in different directions. Prioritizing time with Jesus might seem impossible, but if we are to reflect His light, we need intentional time in His presence. Time spent with Jesus helps us refocus our thoughts from our tasks to the people we love.

Today lay down your list at the feet of Jesus. Ask Him what He would have you remove from your list so you have the freedom to be a reflection of His light today. In time spent with Him, He refreshes you spiritually and physically. He changes your priorities, infusing you with the light of the Holy Spirit—then you are more available to share His love with others.

The more our relationship grows with Jesus, the brighter His light shines in and through us, so we become a vessel of His light and love to our families. Jesus didn't create us to meet worldly expectations but for living life focused on loving Him and the people in our lives.

# *Prayer*

*Dear Jesus, I want this Christmas to be different. Fill me with the desire to prioritize time with the people I love. I don't want exhaustion and lists as my priority. As I spend time with you, change my heart, help me to value relationships, and be a shining light of your love today.*

**❝** Quietness and prayer are essential for our spiritual growth and emotional well-being. **❞**

# Silence

*Be still before the Lord and wait
patiently for him. For God alone,
my soul waits in silence.*

(Psalm 37:7; 62:1 ESV)

I surround myself with Christmas music to fill the quiet with background noise. The music drowns out my mile-a-minute thoughts over all my holiday preparations. I don't want to be alone with my thoughts and take the time to process their underlying cause. (Hmm...perfection, people pleasing, ...) Even my morning time with God has become possessed by distraction. Ending my day overstimulated and cranky, I snap with frustration at my family. I know I need some space for quiet with God to ease my tension, but I lack the follow-through. Without my daily connection in His presence, I'm walking on a tight rope, ready to fall.

Do you remember the last time you had a moment of pure silence?

Quieting our thoughts and finding joy in silence is a struggle. And yet by stopping and being present with our thoughts, we give ourselves the necessary space for our thoughts to be put at rest in the presence of God. In the quiet, the voice of the Lord reaches through our distracted minds and turns our focus back to Him.

Jesus understood the importance of creating a quiet space in His day for prayer. He experienced the same daily demands of life, so I imagine it was difficult for Him to quiet His mind in the silence. Jesus understands our inability to hear Him above the noise; this is one of the reasons He modeled the daily practice of drawing away for prayer in a place of silence and being replenished by His Father. Quietness and prayer are essential for our spiritual growth and emotional well-being.

Practicing the art of silence allows God's infusion of light, giving us a fresh perspective on our lives. He knows we need the stillness and quiet, especially at Christmas, to refocus and reconnect with Him. He understands it's difficult to shut out the noise.

Be creative about finding a space for quiet. Find a room and close the door. Set a timer for ten minutes and be physically still in His presence. Pray, "Lord, help me quiet my mind." Experience waves of His love washing over you. If your mind wanders, refocus, and say aloud, "God, here I am, I wish to be with you." Then be silent again. Though it may be awkward, persevere. He will bless your time together with new insights into Himself and you. All He asks is for you to come.

# Prayer

*Lord, I am grateful you model the practice of prayer in a quiet place. I struggle with stillness, both physically and mentally, in your presence. Help me quiet my mind and be present with you. I desire your perspective on my day, and I seek to glorify you with my choices and words.*

" Walking by faith
takes bold moves
and intentionality. "

# Participation

believe

19

> He replied, "Because you have so little faith.
> Truly I tell you, if you have faith as small as
> a mustard seed, you can say to this mountain,
> 'Move from here to there,' and it will move.
> Nothing will be impossible for you."
>
> (Matthew 17:20 NIV)

I slowly ease my car through the slick parking lot, only to encounter a mountain of snow blocking my view of oncoming traffic. Frustrated, I realize there isn't an easier way out. Hoping there isn't another car coming, I cautiously move my car forward, inch by inch, peering beyond the massive pile. Finally, a quarter of the way into the crossroads, I sigh in relief; the coast is clear. I am grateful I have avoided a collision.

Faith is not always tangible, nor is my spiritual journey. At times I swear there is a mountain blocking my spiritual growth. That's why I find it helpful to pause and reflect on my faith at Christmas. I have experienced seasons when I'm flying on a spiritual high, confident of God's direction and equipping. In other seasons, I'm inching forward, cautiously peering around the corner, waiting for God to move.

Are you inching along spiritually, wondering what is around the corner?

We have a part to play in our spiritual growth. We can't sit back, expecting God to do all the heavy lifting. It takes time, regular practice, and perseverance to grow and apply what God is teaching us. He's given us His Word, prayer, and the Holy Spirit to guide and teach us. With God on our side and a little faith, we can move any mountain blocking our view and grow spiritually.

Walking by faith takes bold moves and intentionality. Spending time in prayer and reading His Word provides a clearer picture of God's faithfulness. He is trustworthy and helps us along the way. Don't let today go by without reading your Bible and praying. Open His Word right now and ask Him for the Holy Spirit's help in growing your faith. Read about the heroes of our faith in Hebrews 11, but today, choose to read in a translation of the Bible you don't normally use.

Every time we are intentional about connecting with God through prayer and reading the Word, our faith is strengthened. This then helps us move one step at a time in the direction God leads. Through our prayer and action, He equips us to face the day and whatever mountain may be in front of us.

# Prayer

*Jesus, the mountains in front
of me are overwhelming,
and I'd rather sit back and
wait on you to do the heavy
lifting. Increase my desire for
spending time in your presence.
Teach me about who you are
so that my faith increases.*

**" God's outstretched arms are waiting to pull you into His loving embrace. "**

# Outstretched Arms

*Hear me as I pray, O Lord. Be merciful and answer me! My heart has heard you say, "Come and talk with me." And my heart responds, "Lord, I am coming."*

(Psalm 27:7–8)

There is a chill in the air as I glance out the window. Today, I am blessed to spend the day with my granddaughter. I never thought I would be the type of grandma who frequently glances out the window to see if she's arrived, but I can't help myself. My heart is full of love for this little one, and I can't wait to spend time with her. Finally, they arrive. As my granddaughter gets out of the van, I call her name. She turns, face erupting in pure joy, and runs, arms outstretched in my direction, eager to receive my embrace and be gathered in my arms.

Like me, with Christmas only a few days away, you may be pushing yourself to finish your preparations. Wrapping gifts, cleaning, and baking can throw us into a frenzy. As we struggle to balance our wants with our needs, we miss the important moments of joy offered in God's presence.

An embrace from someone who loves us releases endorphins of joy. Our bodies relax as we nestle into the comfort of the embrace. Our mood is lifted, and we are reminded of the importance of spending time with others. A single hug, received or given, changes our perspective on what is truly necessary at Christmas.

Do you need God's loving embrace today?

Instead of getting wrapped up in your "wants," God desires you to spend time with Him and those you love. His outstretched arms are waiting to pull you into His loving embrace. Imagine Him scooping you up and lifting you high in the air. His whole being overflowing with love, excitement, and joy as He watches you run in His direction with abandon.

Today, set some boundaries on your time. Turn off worldly noise and social media notifications and spend time talking with the God who loves you. Close your eyes and experience a tight embrace from His mighty arms. God's eyes are bursting with love! Let His love wash over you, allow the tension to seep from your body. Surrender your remaining preparations to His care and allow Him to show you which are truly necessary.

# *Prayer*

*Jesus, I confess, my preparations
have pushed thoughts of you from
my mind. I am grateful you call
me even though I neglect our
relationship. I need your help today
and want to put my relationships
first. Help me see those around me
who need an embrace from my arms.*

" Jesus' love envelops us, infusing us with contentment and joy. "

# Joy

*Jesus called the children to him and said,
"Let the little children come to me, and do
not hinder them, for the kingdom of God
belongs to such as these."*

(Luke 18:16 NIV)

Tired and slightly stressed after a long day at work, I
need some fresh air to decompress and burn off steam.
Bundling up, my husband and I head out to enjoy the
snow. As soon as we step outside, the kid in me takes
over. I can't help but grab a handful of snow, compact
it, and surprise my husband with a snowball to his back.
Snow cascades down his neck as he turns in my direction
with a smirk on his face. The child in both of us comes
out as we engage in a full-scale snowball fight. Covered
in snow, tears running down our cheeks, we gasp for air,
laughing uncontrollably—the laughter a needed release
and a great way to add joy at the end of our week.

When was the last time you laughed so hard you
cried and your face hurt?

Pure joy is often found when we shake off the constraints of adulthood and enjoy God's creation. Sometimes dusting off the child within helps us fully experience the majesty of what God created for our pleasure. Approaching God with childlike wonder, we see Him through new eyes and are quicker to believe in and trust Him.

Jesus welcomed children, even when He was at His busiest. He recognized their faith and the joy they experienced in life. The children came with no pretenses or expectations. He greeted them, drawing them close. He gave them His full attention, and they found joy and love in His arms.

When we turn and look at Jesus with the eyes of a child, His love envelops us, infusing us with contentment and joy. Our countenance changes and others wonder where our joy and peace are coming from. This gives us the opportunity to share how our joy comes from Jesus.

Shake off the constraints of adulthood for a little while today. Put aside your need to have everything completed and do something that brings you joy. Play a game, knit, or read a book. Whatever brings you joy, thank God for creating you for experiencing the joy in life and in Him.

# Prayer

*Jesus, thank you for the joy you
bring into my life. Help me put
aside my adult expectations as I
come to you with the faith of a child.
Fill me with your joy and love today.
As I walk with you, I pray your love
flows through me as I share your
light and love with those in my life.*

“ Time with Jesus
enriches our lives. ”

# Enriches

*May the Lord make your love for one
another and for all people grow and overflow,
just as our love for you overflows.*

(1 Thessalonians 3:12)

As evening approaches, my mind churns with thoughts of Christmas's busy schedule. I have too much on my plate and no time to decompress. Having wrapped up most of my planning for Christmas, I long for connection. Calling a friend, we schedule breakfast for tomorrow morning. Our time together is exactly what I need. We encourage one another, laughing at our attempts to create the perfect holiday. My body relaxes, releasing its tension. I am grateful for friends who help me refocus on what's important—loving others. We are blessed by our relationship and how it has enriched each other's lives.

Do you need some time to decompress and refocus?

Stepping away from what consumes our day brings us a fresh perspective. Spending time with a good friend sheds light on our intentions, helping us laugh at our attempts to create a specific image. With their loving insights, we can reverse course, focusing on the important relationships in our lives.

Spending time with Jesus helps us decompress and sheds light on our intentions as well. He loves us, knows our tendencies, and desires only the best for us. His guidance and loving correction shift our focus to help us love Him and the people in our lives. Time with Him enriches our lives.

As my relationship with Jesus grows, He is enriching my life, helping me find joy no matter my circumstances. He is eager to listen at a moment's notice and provides insight and guidance in the choices I make each day. He reminds me daily of His presence and love. Using the exploding colors of a sunset or sunrise, He reminds me He is actively pursuing me. He has my best interests in mind, and He loves me unconditionally, gently pointing out where I need to make changes. I am blessed by His love for me and by our growing relationship.

Today, create some space to decompress with Jesus. Ask Him to reveal any areas in your life where you've created unrealistic expectations. Make a list of how you've seen His presence in your life, enriching it as only He can. Pray over the list you've created, giving thanks for all He has done for you. Now ask Him whose life you could enrich today. Write their name down and pray for them.

# *Prayer*

*Jesus, thank you for your patience with me when I create unrealistic expectations. I am grateful for friends who make me laugh at my choices. May I love those in my life well, following your example. Help me reach out to _____, whom you brought to mind. Give me wisdom in loving them well.*

" Thankfulness deepens
our connection to the Vine
and increases our joy. "

# The Vine

> *Yes, I am the vine; you are the branches.*
> *Those who remain in me, and I in them,*
> *will produce much fruit. For apart from*
> *me you can do nothing. I have told you*
> *these things so that you will be filled with*
> *my joy. Yes, your joy will overflow! This is*
> *my commandment: Love each other in the*
> *same way I have loved you.*
>
> (John 15:5, 11–12)

Christmas is two days away, and I have a few last minute things to complete. I inhale deeply and exhale. Closing my eyes, I give thanks for what has been accomplished. This season, my goal has been to be intentional about spending time with those I love. I pray I've succeeded. Releasing my list into God's hands, I take another cleansing breath and ask, "Lord, where shall I focus my energies today?" I sense Him saying, *Choose love.*

Every day has endless choices. Cleaning, groceries, taking the kids to the park, TV, radio, what to make for dinner. . . If we listed them all, it would be overwhelming.

Christmas adds another dimension to our choices, making it difficult to zero in on what is truly necessary for the day.

How do we weed through the endless choices before us, keeping our focus on God and the people we love?

When we are connected to the One who loves and created us, He helps us sift through the choices so we can focus on our loved ones. Just as grapes must stay connected to the vine to grow, we need the same connection with God to flourish. Through reading our Bibles, prayer, and worship, He reminds us we are called to love others as He loves us.

Knowing who we are in Christ brings a fresh perspective on loving others like Christ loves us. As the Holy Spirit fills us with new insights into Christ's love, we can express our gratitude through prayer. Thankfulness deepens our connection to the Vine and increases our joy.

Today, reflect on Christ's love for you and the many ways He's involved in your life. Praise Him and give thanks. Inhale deeply, imagining your inhalation as a signal of the Holy Spirit alive within you. Focus on John 15 and allow Jesus' words to soothe your soul. His Word is a precious gift, His love story to you.

# Prayer

*Jesus, I am grateful you promise
that as we stay connected to you,
our joy will overflow. Thank you
for the gift of the Holy Spirit, who
teaches me how to love others as
you love me. Help me pull the weeds
out from my day so I am available
to love those I encounter today.*

" There's peace and rest
found in the home of Jesus. "

# Home

*The Word became flesh and made his
dwelling among us. We have seen his glory,
the glory of the one and only Son, who came
from the Father, full of grace and truth.*

(John 1:14 NIV)

Wriggling in their seats, the kids pester, "How long until
we get there?" We're spending a week with our family
for Christmas. At first disappointed they weren't going
to be home for the holidays, now they can hardly wait to
see their cousins. It's all they've talked about for the last
week. My husband and I are just as eager. As a family
we're spread out all over the country, and it's been far
too long since we've all been together in one place. It's
much easier connecting face-to-face and expressing our
love for one another in the same room.

Home is where your heart is. For many of us, our child-
hood home is no longer. Parents have moved, retired, or
passed away. Home no longer feels like "home." When we
visit, we're unsettled, as if we've lost a piece of our history.
As family traditions change, tension often develops in

93

our relationships. It helps if we remind ourselves that the essence of home isn't between a specific four walls but is found in a room full of people who love one another.

What changes are causing you to feel unsettled today?

I wonder if Jesus felt unsettled when He began His ministry. He left the comforts of His earthly home behind and traveled from place to place with His disciples, each day bringing different challenges. His home became wherever God called Him to share the Good News. As Jesus shared His message of love, hope, and forgiveness, He was pointing people to their eternal home in heaven.

Jesus recognizes your desire for a foundational place to call home. He offers this through a personal relationship with Him. His home provides security and love. When you accept Him as your Lord and Savior, He makes His home within you. Jesus gives you the gift of the Holy Spirit to guide your steps and equip you for the life before you.

There's peace and rest found in the home of Jesus. Bring your unsettled emotions to Him. Close your eyes and imagine yourself outside His home. Release the stressors of your life. Allow the tension to ease from your body. Breathe. The door is opening. His hand is outstretched, welcoming you. He kisses you on both cheeks, His smile reflecting His love: "Come, my child, join me. What's troubling you?"

# Prayer

*Jesus, thank you for giving me a home. You love and welcome me, even when I stray from your presence. Help me release my definition of what makes a home. As I gather with my family this Christmas, may I boldly share your love with them today.*

God refreshes
our soul and fills
us with joy.

# Rejoice

*A child is born to us, a son is given to us. The government will rest on his shoulders. And he will be called: Wonderful Counselor, Mighty God, Everlasting Father, Prince of Peace.*

(Isaiah 9:6)

Opening my eyes, I beam with excitement. Christmas day is here. I am filled with gratitude. God has infused me with a peaceful spirit. He's refreshed my soul and filled me with joy. My stress levels are lower, my body is relaxed, and my mind at ease.

I shouldn't be surprised. As I prioritized my time, spending it with the Lord, He helped me realign my heart. My focus turned from my preparations to the people I love. It wasn't always easy. Some days I got wrapped up in all my preparations, pushing off my time to connect with the Lord, never quite following through. Yet when I started my day in His presence, I found it easier to keep my eyes fixed on Him. I am thankful for His faithfulness and reminders of His love and mercy when I chose to focus elsewhere.

I hope you've woken today well rested and peaceful. As you've spent less time focusing on your holiday preparations and more time with God, I pray your intimacy with God has grown and flourished. I also hope you've found joy in loving the people in your life. I pray, as life returns to "normal," you'll continue making time with Jesus a priority.

Merry Christmas!

Thank you for joining me on this journey as we've sought joy and love in the presence of Jesus and refocused our hearts on the people we love.

# Prayer

*Lord Jesus, I love you. Thank you for teaching me what it means to have a relationship with you. Thank you for showing me how to love people well. Your love and faithfulness fill me with awe. I pray I continue to set aside time each day to spend in your presence. Amen.*

# About the Author

Julie became passionate about reading her Bible when she noticed a direct correlation between her ability to love well and how many days per week she took time to read God's Word. This created in her a desire for others to encounter the joy she found in a life with Jesus. This desire, prompted by God, culminated in blogging her thoughts as God continued revealing to her a new way of living and thinking. This book is a compilation of God's insight into her everyday life.

As she continued to learn and grow from God's Word, she began to undergo a deeper sense of peace and joy in her life. She didn't know it at the time, but God was preparing her for some difficulties on the horizon: three different bouts with cancer, losing her only kidney, and receiving a kidney transplant. Through all the uncertainties, God continues to be faithful and help her live life filled with joy and peace that is only found through an intimate relationship with Him. God has shown her that today's challenges are His way of preparing her for tomorrow's adventure.

Julie lives in Northern Illinois with her husband Maurice. She has a love for the outdoors, no matter the weather. Seeing God through His creation fuels her creative spirit. Weather permitting, you will find her sitting by the lake as she writes, enjoying the lapping sound of the water against the shore and listening for God's direction. She is blessed to be a grandmother and is constantly amazed to see life through the eyes of her grandchildren. In the eyes of a child, one can truly see God.

Julie invites you to join her on the adventure of following Jesus. You can find her at:

🌐 www.julieademe.com

📘 facebook.com/JulieAdeme.Author

📷 @julieademe